From Wood to Paper

From Wood to Paper

Ali Mitgutsch

 Carolrhoda Books, Inc., Minneapolis

First published in the United States of America 1986 by Carolrhoda Books, Inc.
Original edition © 1982 by Sellier Verlag GmbH, Eching bei München,
West Germany, under the title VOM HOLZ ZUM PAPIER.
Revised English text © 1986 by Carolrhoda Books, Inc.
Illustrations © 1982 by Sellier Verlag GmbH.
All rights reserved.

Manufactured in the United States of America

LIBRARY OF CONGRESS CATALOGING-IN-PUBLICATION DATA

Mitgutsch, Ali.
From wood to paper.

(A Carolrhoda start to finish book)
Translation of: Vom Holz zum Papier.
Summary: Describes the individual steps taken in
making wood into paper and what happens to the finished
product.

1. Paper—Juvenile literature. 2. Wood—Juvenile
literature. [1. Papermaking. 2. Paper] I. Title.
II. Series.

TS1105.5.M5613   1986   676'.2   86-17177
ISBN 0-87614-296-X (lib. bdg.)

1 2 3 4 5 6 7 8 9 10 96 95 94 93 92 91 90 89 88 87 86

From Wood to Paper

People have been using paper for many centuries.
For much of this time, paper was made from rags.
Today, most paper is made from wood.
Every year, many new trees must be planted
to replace the ones that have been cut down
for making paper.
Some of these trees will be cut down
and sold as Christmas trees.
Other trees are allowed to grow much taller
before they are cut down.
These very tall trees will be cut down and made into paper.

First the trees are cut into logs
of exactly the same length.
Then the bark is taken off.
Bark would make dark spots in the paper.
A machine then grinds the wood into tiny chips
that are almost as fine as powder.

A huge machine mixes the wood powder with water
to make a paste.
This machine has beaters
just like an electric cake mixer.

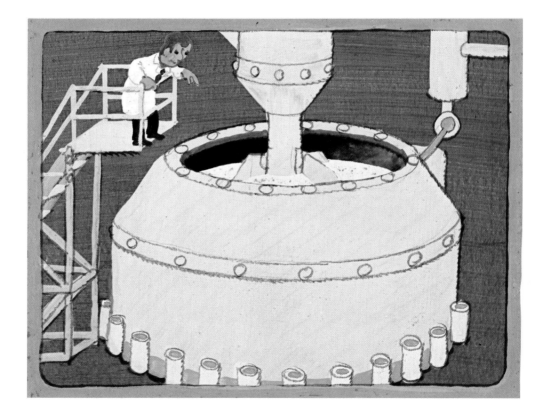

The wood paste is then poured into another machine along with some glue.
The glue helps make the paper strong so that it will be hard to tear.
Cellulose, which is another product made from wood, is added to the paste.
Cellulose is a substance that is found in most plants.
It is made of tiny fibers.
These fibers form the paper.
The cellulose is dropped into the paste from a conveyor belt.

The soft, wet paper paste is poured onto a moving screen
called a **sieve.**
Most of the water drips out through the sieve.
The moist paper then comes out of the sieve
and runs onto hot rollers.

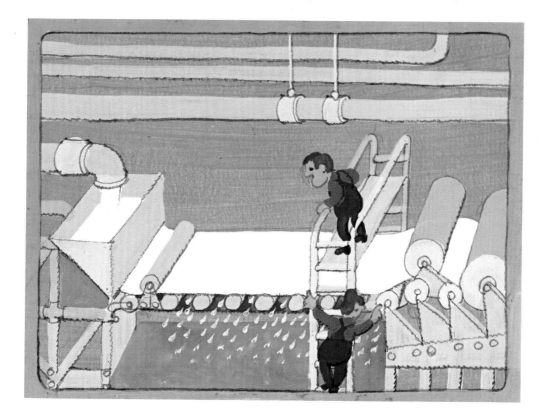

The rollers work like giant irons.
The moist paper is squeezed through them,
and the paper becomes smooth, thin, and dry.
Paper-making machines are some of the
longest machines in the world.
Many are longer than two football fields put together.

The finished paper is wound up into huge, heavy rolls. Later it will be trimmed into many different sizes. The trimmed sheets of paper are stored in warehouses until they are needed.

Many, many tons of paper are printed every day
and sold as books, newspapers, or magazines.
Drawing paper, tissues, toilet paper, money, and many other
products we use everyday are made from paper, too.

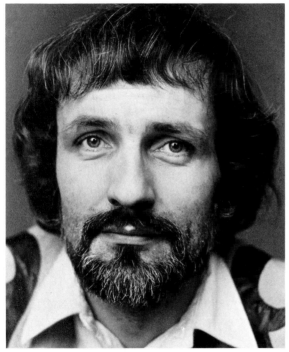

Ali
Mitgutsch

ALI MITGUTSCH is one of Germany's best-known children's book illustrators. He is a devoted world traveler, and many of his book ideas have taken shape during his travels. Perhaps this is why they have such international appeal. Mr. Mitgutsch's books have been published in 22 countries and are enjoyed by thousands of readers around the world.

Ali Mitgutsch lives with his wife and three children in Schwabing, the artists' quarter in Munich. The Mitgutsch family also enjoys spending time on their farm in the Bavarian countryside.

THE CAROLRHODA
>>> START

From Beet to Sugar	From Grass to Butter
NEW From Blueprint to House	From Ice to Rain
From Blossom to Honey	NEW From Lemon to Lemonade
From Cacao Bean to Chocolate	From Milk to Ice Cream
From Cement to Bridge	From Oil to Gasoline
From Clay to Bricks	From Ore to Spoon
From Cotton to Pants	NEW From Rubber Tree to Tire
From Cow to Shoe	From Sand to Glass
From Dinosaurs to Fossils	From Sea to Salt
From Egg to Bird	From Seed to Pear
From Egg to Butterfly	From Sheep to Scarf
From Fruit to Jam	From Swamp to Coal
From Gold to Money	From Tree to Table
From Grain to Bread	NEW From Wood to Paper
From Graphite to Pencil	

TO FINISH >>>
BOOKS

0(